Wildfire!

BY ELIZABETH RAUM

AMICUS HIGH INTEREST • AMICUS INK

Amicus High Interest and Amicus Ink are imprints of Amicus
P.O. Box 1329, Mankato, MN 56002
www.amicuspublishing.us

Library of Congress Cataloging-in-Publication Data
Raum, Elizabeth, author.
Wildfire! / by Elizabeth Raum.
     pages cm. – (Natural disasters)
Audience: K to grade 3.
Summary: "This photo-illustrated book describes wildfires,
including forest fires, grass fires, and bush fires. Explains how
these fires are started, what conditions create a crisis, and steps
taken to put fires out. Also includes information on staying safe
and preventing wildfires"– Provided by publisher.
ISBN 978-1-60753-993-3 (library binding) – ISBN 978-1-
68152-086-5 (pbk.) – ISBN 978-1-60753-999-5 (ebook)
1. Wildfires–Juvenile literature. 2. Wildfires–Prevention and
control–Juvenile literature. I. Title.
SD421.23.R38 2017
363.37'9–dc23

                                2015033737

Editor: Wendy Dieker
Series Designer: Kathleen Petelinsek
Book Designer: Tracy Myers
Photo Researcher: Rebecca Bernin

Photo Credits: mironov/Shutterstock cover; J. Emilio Flores/
Getty 4-5; Rick D'Elia/Corbis 6; Sandy Huffaker/Getty 9; Alex
Coppel/National Geographic My Shot/National Geographic
Creative 10; Rick D'Elia/Corbis 13; alacatr/iStock 14; Max
Whittaker/Reuters/Corbis 17; Mike McMillan/Spotfire Images
18; Michael Turcotte/Alamy Stock Photo 21; Rick Wilking/
Reuters/Corbis 22; Jim Brandenburg/Minden Pictures/
National Geographic Creative 24-25; David McNew/Getty
26; Craig Durling/Zuma Press/Corbis 29

Printed in the United States of America.

HC 10 9 8 7 6 5 4 3 2 1
PB 10 9 8 7 6 5 4 3 2 1

Table of Contents

Smoke!   4

Bad Burns   8

Fighting Wildfires   **16**

Dealing with Wildfires   20

Staying Safe   **27**

Glossary   30

Read More   31

Websites   31

Index   **32**

Smoke!

Smoke fills the air. It is hard to breathe. The fire is getting closer to your neighborhood. You have to leave. Neighbors are leaving, too. You stay in a safe place until the fire is out. When you go home, you see the fire damage. The fire burned homes, cars, and trees. It is a sad sight.

Wildfires create huge smoke clouds.

Heat from lightning strikes can start a wildfire.

 Is a forest fire the same thing as a wildfire?

About 100,000 wildfires happen in the U.S. every year. They happen all over the world, too. Every fire needs heat, **fuel**, and **oxygen** to burn. This is called the **fire triangle**. Heat, such as lightning or matches, can start a fire. Fuel, such as trees or grass, feeds the fire. And **oxygen**, which is in the air, keeps it burning.

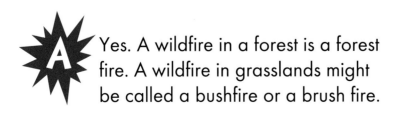 Yes. A wildfire in a forest is a forest fire. A wildfire in grasslands might be called a bushfire or a brush fire.

Bad Burns

Some wildfires are small. Firefighters put them out quickly. Others burn for weeks. If a strong wind blows, the fire spreads quickly. Wildfires destroy trees and plants. They kill animals. They burn homes. They kill people. Sometimes wildfires strike forests. Other times, they burn grasslands. A wildfire can happen anywhere.

Firefighters battle a raging blaze in Southern California. They help keep it from spreading.

Smoke clouds from the bushfires in Australia completely hide the sky.

 What caused the Black Saturday Bushfires?

One of the worst wildfire events happened in Australia in February 2009. At least 47 different fires began burning. They were called the Black Saturday Bushfires. Strong winds carried flames over highways and up hills. The fires became giant fireballs. People did not have time to escape. The fires killed 173 people. More than 400 people were injured.

 The worst fire began with a spark from an electrical pole. The weather was hot and dry. That made the fires spread very quickly.

In May 2011, a campfire started a wildfire in Bear Wallow Wilderness area in Arizona. The area was very dry. There were strong winds. The fire spread to New Mexico. It burned for about six weeks. Fire destroyed 29 homes. Smoke spread north over many states as far away as Wisconsin. The smoke made it difficult to breathe.

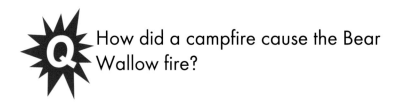

Q How did a campfire cause the Bear Wallow fire?

Firefighters work to stop the Bear Wallow fire from spreading.

 When the campers left, they did not put their fire out. The fire jumped to the dry grass and quickly got out of control.

The California wildfire in 2013 left little more than charred tree trunks in the forest.

 Will this California forest recover from the fire?

In August 2013, a huge fire began in a California canyon. High winds spread the fire into the dry forest. The fire burned more than 410 square miles (660 sq km) of land. It burned trees. Many animals died. Some rare animals lost their homes. The forest was home to great gray owls, rare red foxes, and Pacific fisher weasels.

 The U.S. Forest Service says it may take 200 years to regrow the forest.

Fighting Wildfires

A good way to fight a wildfire is to take away the fuel. A **firebreak** is an area with no fuel. Firefighters called hotshots cut down trees. They clear away brush. They use bulldozers and tractors to clear the land. The firebreak is wide. Fire cannot jump over the cleared area. Rivers, ponds, and lakes also act as firebreaks.

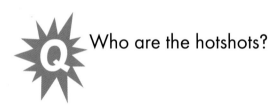 Who are the hotshots?

Firefighters called hotshots clear the area in the path of a fire to prevent its spreading.

 A They are brave men and women who fight wildfires. They study fire science and first aid. They spend hours training to fight fires.

Smokejumpers jump out of planes
to start fighting the wildfire.

 **Q** Who sets **backfires**?

Backfires help control wildfires. Backfires are small fires that burn toward the wildfire. When the fires meet, they die out. The fuel is all burned up.

Helicopters fly over the wildfires. They drop water on fires. So do planes called **air tankers**. Air tankers also drop red stuff on the fire. It is **retardant**. It slows and cools the fire.

 Hotshots and smokejumpers do. Smokejumpers are firefighters who jump out of airplanes. They also help build firebreaks.

Dealing with Wildfires

Lightning starts about 1 in 10 wildfires. People start the rest. They fail to put out campfires correctly. They toss a match into leaves. They let leaf or grass fires get out of control. Sometimes people start fires on purpose. That is called **arson**. Setting fires on purpose is against the law.

 How should you put out a campfire?

Campfires can quickly get out of control in dry places. Campers should take fire safety seriously.

 Pour water on the fire until it stops hissing. Stir the ashes with a shovel. Make sure everything is wet and cool.

Tall grass, weeds, and dead leaves are fuel for fires. People who live in an area where wildfires are common keep their yards clear. They remove dead plants, grass, and weeds. They rake dry leaves and pine needles and remove dead tree branches. Many towns collect yard waste. This helps prevent wildfires.

This woman clears her yard of dried plants that could be fuel for a wildfire.

Wildfires are dangerous. Fires destroy the homes of animals and people. But scientists know fires can be good for the land. Fires clear out dead plants. They kill bugs that infest trees. They can even cause new growth. Some trees have seedpods that only open in high heat. And burned plants leave nutrients in the soil that make it healthy.

Ashes from burned trees make good soil for new growth.

People leave their homes before a fire reaches the area.

 Q How will I know if there's a fire nearby?

Staying Safe

If there's a wildfire, the police may order everyone to leave the area. It's smart to have an emergency kit ready. Grab it. Leave right away.

If you are hiking or camping, don't try to run. Wade into a pond or river. If there is no water nearby, lie down in a cleared ditch. Breathe the air near the ground.

 You will smell smoke in the air. Radio and TV stations will report news about it.

Nature needs fire to refresh and regrow. But fires that get out of control can kill people and animals. They can burn down homes. A big wildfire can do more than $1 billion in damage. It's important to be safe with fire.

A deer runs away as a wildfire burns its home.

Glossary

air tanker A plane that drops water or retardant on a wildfire.

arson The act of setting a fire on purpose; arson is against the law.

backfire A fire set by firefighters to stop a wildfire.

firebreak Land cleared of fuel to help stop a fire.

fire triangle The three things needed by a fire: heat, fuel, and oxygen.

fuel A material that will burn and keep a fire going.

oxygen An odorless, colorless gas found in air.

retardant Something that stops or slows a fire or other event.

Read More

Baltzer, Rochelle. *Wildfires*. Edina, Minn.: ABDO Pub Co., 2012.

Bond, Rebecca. *Out of the Woods: A True Story of an Unforgettable Event*. New York: Margaret Ferguson Books, 2015.

Goldish, Meish. *Smoke Jumpers*. New York: Bearport Publishing, 2014.

Websites

Dialogue for Kids | Wildfires
http://idahoptv.org/dialogue4kids/season3/wildfires/facts.cfm

Only You Can Prevent Wildfires
http://www.smokeybear.com/kids/?js=1

Weather WizKids | Wildfires
http://www.weatherwizkids.com/weather-wildfire.htm

Index

air tankers 19

animals 8, 15, 24, 28

Arizona 12

arson 20

Australia 11

backfires 18, 19

Bear Wallow
 Wilderness fire 12, 13

Black Saturday
 Bushfires 10, 11

bushfires 7, 10, 11

California 14, 15

campfires 13, 20

causes 7, 10, 11, 12,
 13, 20

firebreaks 16, 19

fire triangle 7

forest fires 6, 7, 8, 14,
 15

hotshots 16, 19

New Mexico 12

oxygen 7

preventing wildfires 20,
 21, 23

regrowth 14, 15, 24, 28

retardant 19

safety 4, 27, 28

smokejumpers 19

About the Author

Elizabeth Raum has worked as a teacher, librarian, and writer. She says, "Storms are exciting." She has lived through blizzards and floods. She's seen a tornado in the distance. She watched earthquakes, hurricanes, and wildfires on the Weather Channel. It's safer! Visit her website at www.elizabethraum.net.